Leadership
STARTS WITH
YOU*

TIM MILBURN

LEADERSHIP STARTS WITH YOU / Tim Milburn
ISBN 9781469912646

www.leadershipstartswithyou.com

For Travis, Tori, Mitch, & Abby

You all inspire me to keep learning how to lead myself better.

✳ ✳ ✳
CONTENTS

"Nothing so conclusively proves a man's ability to lead others as what he does from day to day to lead himself."

-- Thomas Watson --

THE ONE THING
YOU NEED TO KNOW

Leadership starts with you.

It doesn't start with a position. Nor with a promotion.
It doesn't start with your first follower or your second
follower.

Leadership starts with the person you must lead first. That
person is you. Before you lead anyone else you first lead
you.

Because, when others decide to follow you, before they
fall in line behind your leadership, they want to see if you
can lead you.

We, the people, have had enough. We've seen one too
many step into a position of leadership only to fall or fail
because they never took the time necessary to lead the
most important person of all - themselves.

Successful leadership is always preceded
by self-leadership.

If you aspire to lead then I'm talking to you. Self-leadership is required each and every day. I urge you to take some of your time, your energy, your resources and invest them in yourself. When you wake up in the morning until you put your head on the pillow at night, self-leadership informs the decisions you are making about you. You're choosing to be a better person or to be the same person.

YOU LEADING YOU = YOU INVESTING IN YOU.

This sounds selfish. *It isn't.*
This sounds arrogant. *Yet it's one of the most humbling acts.*
This sounds like a waste of time. *Then don't lead.*

It's difficult to be a great leader if you can't be great at leading yourself. Too many step into a position of leadership and do not make self-leadership a priority. When that happens, they're not in leadership for very long. They burn out or they implode. They end up making an error in judgment or behavior they can't recover from.

And at the end of the day, they're right back to square one. So, the lesson is: **With no one following, the only person left to influence is yourself.**

That sounds like a great place to start.

This book is a chance to look in the mirror. It's all about learning to lead the person you see there. At times, the person in the reflection will be excited and motivated to follow your leadership. But there will be moments when he or she will push back. You would think that leading oneself would be easy. I mean, it's only me leading me. Yet the me inside will resist, will rationalize, will argue about almost anything.

This book isn't long. It's not hard to read. You can knock the whole thing out in a couple of hours. But the ideas and the issues it raises take a lifetime to develop.

You leading you is the entrance exam to you leading others.

If you pass the test of leading yourself well on a daily basis, you'll find you can advance to the next stage of leading others well. But you can't skip this class. If you do, you'll become a hollow leader. You'll lack depth and credibility. Your words will be shallow. Your influence will lack substance.

There's a familiar speech given thousands of times a day. It's spoken on airplanes around the world. The flight attendant stands in front of a captive, yet often distracted audience, and delivers the precautionary safety instructions. At some point, passengers are shown a demonstration on the proper way to use the oxygen mask should there be a sudden change in cabin pressure. The teachable moment comes when the flight attendant instructs those flying with small children to put their mask on first, and then place the mask over the child.

Of course, this sounds so self-serving, if not downright cruel. Save the child! We're ready to sacrifice ourselves for the good of the kid. But the wisdom of this process is simple: If you're not breathing, you can't help anyone else breathe. It may not seem obvious to you, but you're of more use to the child *conscious* then you are passed out from a lack of oxygen (unconscious people aren't very helpful).

But don't stop there. Think about this principle. It's not just putting on the oxygen mask first so the child can breathe. That's a hypothetical at this point. This child needs you. He or she needed you to help put on a seat belt. Before that you helped this child find his or her seat. Before that you helped this child know the correct gate to get on the correct plane. Before that you helped this child get through the security line. Before that you drove this child to the airport. Before that you bought a plane ticket for this child so you both could travel. Before that you helped this child get up and dressed and fed and prepared to go.

The bigger story here is that this child is dependent on you to know how to do all of these things. While these concepts may seem simple to you, the child won't be sitting in the seat next to you on the plane without them. The child needs you long before the possibility of cabin depressurization occurs.

That's why I've written this book. **We need you.** The people you lead or may someday lead need you on a regular and consistent basis. We need you to lead yourself well so you can lead others well.

The investment you make in you is actually an investment in those whom you'll influence.

* * *
KEEP THE PROMISES
YOU MAKE TO YOURSELF

Most people live their lives with the best of intentions.

> I'm going to get up an hour earlier tomorrow.
>
> I'm going to use that hour to exercise.
>
> I'm going to eat a healthy breakfast.
>
> I'm going to read that book on my nightstand.
>
> I'm going to write that book on my expertise.
>
> I'm going to spend less and save more.
>
> I'm going to clean up that clutter.
>
> I'm going to spend more time with my kids.

Have you ever made a promise like that?

The thing is, they aren't promises. They're *wishes*.

If they were promises, you'd do your best to keep them.
Instead they're wishes, cleverly masked as promises.

You've taken an image of your ideal self (who you hope
to be) and created a list of wishes that will help you
to become that person. But these statements are not
promises...at least not yet.

We have the intelligence to know what is needed to lead ourselves first and to lead ourselves well. The problem isn't in our heads.

I think it's okay to wish for all kinds of things. Wishes are the seeds from which promises grow. Your wishes are based on your desire to be different, to have something different, to change. Wishes are your imagination taking you to places that don't yet exist in reality. Unfortunately, wishes don't change reality. But promises do...at least the ones we keep.

A promise is an agreement that you will or you won't do something.

We make a variety of promises every day. Most of them we keep, some of them we break.

Why do you break your promises? Have you ever thought about that? I have.

Most of the time it's because of these three things:
1. It's too hard.
2. It hurts.
3. Things change.

Not necessarily rocket science. But that doesn't lessen the reality of each one. Let's break them down one-by-one.

IT'S TOO HARD. We'll make a promise to someone without thinking about all it will take to keep this promise. It turns out to be more work then we envisioned. It ends up costing us more than we thought. It requires a sacrifice we weren't willing to make.

IT HURTS. Sometimes we'll make a promise to someone and then the relationship will take a turn for the worse. If that person hurt me then I'm going to respond in kind and hurt them. I may have made a promise when things were going good, but now that they're going bad, I let myself off the hook.

THINGS CHANGE. Things do change. Circumstances change. Our station in life changes. An unforeseen crisis occurs. And change forces us to adapt with our promises intact or to break them.

Let's be honest - it's hard to keep promises. Both to others and to ourselves. Yet part of what it means to lead ourselves well is keeping the promises we make to ourselves.

If you can't keep the promises you make to yourself, how can you expect to keep the promises you make to others?

When you express a wish, it may or may not happen. In the end it doesn't make much difference - it's just a wish. But a promise is something very different and much more powerful. A promise is a declaration that something will or won't happen. And if you make that declaration and don't follow through, it leads to all kinds of bad things.

- How much do you trust a person who doesn't keep a promise?
- How much do you rely on a person who doesn't keep a promise?
- How much do you want to be led by a person who doesn't keep a promise?

This is why the whole issue of keeping promises has to start with you. It has to start with the promises you make to yourself and then the efforts you make in keeping them.

Those who understand what it means to lead themselves first have learned to make promises to themselves and to keep those promises.

Do you see where self-leadership begins to lay the groundwork for the leadership of others? It's not difficult to make a promise. **What's difficult is learning to manage that promise the next day - to fulfill and keep your promise despite circumstance or crisis.**

If you make a promise to yourself and then don't keep it, that broken promise will slowly tear you apart on the inside, and impact your ability to keep the promises you make to others.

Keeping a promise to yourself gives you the confidence to keep the promises you make to others.

The people who follow you are wondering: *If I can't trust you to keep a promise to yourself, how can I trust you to keep a promise you made to me?*

DISCIPLINE SOUNDS LIKE PUNISHMENT

There's a verse in the Bible that nails this issue. The author is talking about how much he wants to do what is right but can't for some reason. He says: *"I want to do what is good, but I don't. I don't want to do what is wrong, but I do it anyway."* (Romans 7:19)

Ever feel like that?

I think we like to live our lives making wishes instead of promises because it doesn't hurt as much if we don't follow through.

Keeping the promises you make to yourself requires discipline.

That doesn't sound like fun. In fact, when I hear the word discipline my mind immediately goes to images of the woodshed (in my case it was a garage) where my father would teach me the error of my ways with a belt to the backside. Discipline sounds a lot like being grounded or having my privileges taken away.

To be honest...it's kind of like that.

WHEN I CHOOSE TO BE DISCIPLINED IN A CERTAIN AREA OF MY LIFE, I MAKE A PROMISE TO LIVE A CERTAIN WAY, IN A CERTAIN DIRECTION, WITH CERTAIN BEHAVIORS. Discipline takes away some of my options. I can no longer do anything I want. Discipline adds structure to my life. It is the avenue through which I keep my promises.

For example, let's say I want to learn how to play the piano. Lots of people think it would be nice to play the piano. Perhaps they heard someone play the piano and thought to themselves, "I like that. I would like to be able to do that." That, of course, is a wish. There are lots of people in audiences around the world who wish they could play the piano.

But if I turn my wish into a promise, then I change the game. Now I must learn to play the piano. And in order to do that, I will need discipline. The minute I make a promise to learn how to play the piano, I will create a structure in my life that pushes away other options.

Those who wish they could play the piano can't go watch TV or go to the movies. Those who promise to play the piano must stay home and practice. You see...less options.

That's why they call it discipline. I have made a promise to play the piano, but somewhere along the way, I may feel like I don't want to do it anymore. But I do it anyway.

Discipline pushes the emotion out of it. Discipline isn't based on what you feel like doing.

Discipline is what you have to do to keep your promises.

If you want to play the piano, discipline demands you practice the piano. Every day.

It sounds painful. But discipline is what separates the *wish makers* from the *promise keepers*. The good news is, discipline has its own rewards.

If you will keep your promise to yourself about learning to play the piano and follow the demands of discipline to practice every day, there will be a payoff. Someday, somewhere you'll sit down to play the piano. You'll be surrounded by others who will listen and be struck somewhere deep inside them by the beautiful music you are creating with your hands on the keys. When you are done playing, they'll come up to you and say these words, "I wish I could play the piano as beautifully as you."

And you'll smile.

You'll smile because you know there's a difference between a wish and a promise. You'll smile because you made a promise to yourself and you kept that promise through the discipline necessary to become a person who plays the piano and not merely one who wishes they could.

Discipline is the price I pay to keep a promise.

Discipline is the action I need to take on a daily basis to follow through on a promise. Discipline means because I said yes to something, I have also said no to other things.

Sometimes discipline is hard.
Sometimes discipline hurts.
But if I stay disciplined, I'll change and I'll grow.

This is huge when it comes to your leadership. If you can

demonstrate discipline in your own life, you will earn the respect and credibility to expect discipline in the lives of those that follow you.

LEADERSHIP REQUIRES YOU TO LEAD YOURSELF WELL NOT ONLY FOR YOUR SAKE, BUT FOR THE SAKE OF OTHERS. You keep the promises you make to yourself for more than yourself. You make them because they fall in line with what I call, *The Rhodium Rule*.

Have you ever heard of Rhodium? Don't feel bad if you haven't. Not many people have.

Rhodium is a chemical element (chemical symbol Rh and atomic number 45) listed among the most precious metals on earth (in between Platinum and Gold). It is often used as a coating on white gold to improve its luster and on sterling silver to reduce tarnish. It is one of the noble metals, meaning it's highly resistant to the corrosion and oxidation which occur in most base metals. Most of all, Rhodium is extremely rare.

Rhodium is added to other precious metals to help them look better, last longer, and enhance their personal qualities. That's where the rule comes from.

The Rhodium Rule says...

Do unto yourself what will inspire the best in others.

What kind of promises should I make as a leader?

If I follow *The Rhodium Rule* I will make promises not only for my own benefit but for the benefit of others. As I keep my promises, they offer inspiration to those who are trying to keep similar promises.

- I keep a promise to be honest so that it will inspire honesty in others.
- I keep a promise to be physically fit so it will inspire fitness in others.
- I keep a promise to do my work with excellence so it will inspire excellence in others.
- I keep a promise to build healthy relationships so it will inspire healthy relationships in others.
- I keep a promise to keep my promises so it will inspire others to keep their promises.

The Rhodium Rule demonstrates why I keep my promises. **People do what people see.** If I'm not leading myself well, how can I expect those in my care to lead themselves well?

CONSISTENCY

The hardest part of being disciplined is it's so every day.

The key to discipline's power is consistency.

It's doing what's required over and over in a way that leads to depth, improvement, growth, and meaning.

When you lead yourself well you make promises that have an effect on your everyday life. Doing the necessary work (discipline) on a daily basis requires consistency.

YOU CAN'T CRAM FOR DISCIPLINE. When I was a student working on my undergrad degree in Communications I would often put off the big papers until the last minute. Two or three days before they were due, I would quarantine myself into the basement of the library with a small supply of snacks and copious amounts of caffeine, usually in the form of Mountain Dew. Then I would crank out the paper. Sometimes I would do well on the paper, sometimes not. While it's possible to get a paper done this way, it's not the best way.

While cramming may work for writing a term paper, it doesn't work for most other things. Cramming doesn't work for a piano recital. Cramming doesn't work for running a marathon. Cramming doesn't work for losing weight. Cramming doesn't work for building relationships. Cramming doesn't work for effective leadership.

DISCIPLINE CAN'T BE ENGAGED OVER A SHORT PERIOD OF TIME WITH HOPE OF YIELDING GREAT RESULTS IMMEDIATELY. The key to solid discipline is doing the necessary work day in and day out. In a word...consistency.

Consistent discipline is not the same thing as boring repetition. It's not a robotic effort devoid of creativity and nuance. The payoff for your consistency will be growth. Growth means change. Change means different.

Let's go back to the example of playing the piano. You make a promise to learn to play the piano. Discipline requires you to practice. The consistency of discipline is to practice every day. But you're not playing the same thing day after day, week after week, and month after month. The consistent discipline of practicing produces a wonderful reward: improvement. Over time, you are capable of playing harder and more intricate pieces of music. Consistent discipline in the area of playing the piano results in becoming a better piano player.

Some people think consistency is boring but I want to challenge your thinking. In leading yourself well, you must be consistent in your discipline, but that doesn't mean always doing the same exact things in the same exact way.

Consistent discipline can lead to stagnation if you do the same thing over and over again but you never grow or learn or improve.

Learning to lead yourself well means figuring out how to remain consistent in your discipline while improving and stretching in the actions associated with that discipline.

If your promise is to get in better shape, you'll need to consistently work out. But your workout will need to change and adapt as you become more physically fit. You won't see much growth if you consistently do 10 push-ups everyday for a year.

If your promise is to read more, you'll need to consistently find good books and articles. Your reading material will need to change. How much fun would it be if you had to read from the same book everyday?

THE ULTIMATE BENEFIT OF CONSISTENCY IS THAT IT CREATES HABITS. If you are consistent in your discipline, then your actions and thinking will become second nature in that area. You will begin to react naturally in ways that you've trained yourself. When you develop good habits it will have a profound effect on those who follow you.

Consistency in your character develops *integrity*.
Consistency in your attitude creates *trust*.
Consistency in your leadership builds *influence*.

Have you heard of the Chinese bamboo tree? This tree is very different from other trees because it doesn't grow in the usual way. Most trees will grow steadily over time. But the Chinese bamboo tree doesn't even break through the ground during the first four years after planting. You water it, fertilize the ground, care for the soil, and nothing happens. Then, in the fifth year, the tree begins to grow at an astonishing rate. In fact, in a period of just five weeks, a Chinese bamboo tree can grow to a height of 90 feet.

The question is, when did it actually grow?

I've come to the conclusion it grew every day over that period of five to six years. Without the consistent care and nurture it received over the first four years, the Chinese bamboo tree would never have reached its full potential after it sprouted in the fifth year.

Consistent discipline is what fuels *The Rhodium Rule.*

Do unto yourself what will inspire the best in others.

When I engage in leading myself first in a consistent way, keeping my promises, I know that my efforts, at some point, will inspire the efforts of others toward achieving their best.

A leader incorporates *The Rhodium Rule* because he or she understands personal growth leads to growth in others.

GROW YOURSELF

Leaders can't take an interest in growing others if they choose to take an intermission in growing themselves.

Growing old doesn't take a lot of work. You can grow old without even thinking about it. Unfortunately, maturity doesn't come with birthdays.

Learning doesn't happen naturally like aging. Learning takes work. The disciplined kind of work we've been talking about. **People want to follow someone who is self-disciplined, not someone who is self-destructive.** This is why leaders must be learners.

Consider what motivates you to learn and grow. Growing up, you were forced to learn in school. Teachers and tests made us learn something. Some of us did better with books, others with hands-on interaction. Some subjects sparked our interest. In others, we muddled through, hoping for a passing grade.

In school, much of the motivation to learn comes from

outside ourselves - from our teachers. Some teachers are better motivators than others. But there comes a point when you realize that you are the one who is ultimately responsible for your learning. **It's not a question of having teachers, it's a matter of being teachable.**

Just because teaching is taking place doesn't mean learning is happening as well. Teachers have a responsibility to teach. You, as a student, have a responsibility to learn. If you're going to grow, you have to take responsibility for it.

As a keeper of the The Rhodium Rule, your motivation to learn is fueled by your desire to lead. Leaders are learners.

One of the promises you must make to yourself as a leader is that you will stay invested in your learning - the kind of learning that leads to growth. You keep that promise to yourself by taking charge when it comes to your own growth.

Without the structure of an educational system, some leaders lack the ability to identify opportunities to learn and grow. I propose two simple strategies to assist with this process. You can measure and motivate your own growth by looking back and planning ahead.

START BY LOOKING BACK. Take some time to think about your answers to the following questions:

- What were you like a year ago?
- Are you the same person you were then?
- Are you still dealing with the same issues?
- Are you still trying to recover from the same mistakes?
- How many books have you read over the last year?
- How many seminars, conferences, and training events have you attended?
- Do you know any new skills?
- Are your relationships better or worse?
- Have you made any new friends?
- Are you in better or worse shape physically?

Looking back gives you perspective on your personal growth. You can learn a lot from the past if you're willing to take a look at it, reflect on it, evaluate it, and learn from it. Hindsight has something to teach us. Looking at our past shows us why our present is better or worse than it was, say, a year ago.

Evaluating the past is helpful. Living in the past isn't healthy.

Like driving a car, the rear view mirror is a useful tool, but you can't move forward in your vehicle if you're fixated on it. The windshield is a lot bigger than the rear view mirror for a reason. **When it comes to growth, our past may show us where we've been, but it doesn't have to determine where we want to go.**

Personal growth doesn't occur naturally. You must be intentional with it. You can leverage your experiences from the past, learning from mistakes and building on your successes. But looking back is only part of the process. A better way to measure and motivate personal growth is to plan for it. This is the *planning ahead* option.

PLANNING AHEAD IS LIKE THE WINDSHIELD. When you're driving, you stare through the windshield while only glancing at the rear view mirror. You will only move forward in your personal growth to the extent you plan for it and implement that plan. Since you're the one responsible for your growth, you need to create a plan and then follow it.

DO YOU HAVE A GROWTH PLAN? A growth plan is an intentional learning process that results in your personal growth. **You make a promise to keep learning and then make a disciplined plan for it.** The subject matter is up to you. The format is up to you. A growth plan ensures that learning and personal growth happens intentionally rather than incidentally.

If you need help getting started, here's a rough outline for a growth plan using the letters *P.L.A.N.* You will need to fill in the specifics with what's appropriate for you.

P urpose: What do you need to know? Why?

L earning: Where do you want to learn it from? Why?

A ssessment: How will you know you learned it?

N ext Action: What will you do with what you learned?

PURPOSE: What do you need to know and why do you need to know it?

There are all kinds of reasons and motivations for learning. At the start of creating your growth plan, identify what you need to learn and why you need to learn it. People don't stop learning because they run out of things to learn. They stop learning because they lost their drive to learn - learning isn't connected consequence. You're responsible for your own growth. You will remain disciplined and committed if you know your reasons, as well as your resources throughout the learning process.

LEARNING: Where do you want to learn it from?

You can learn from books, the internet, other people, videos, podcasts, classes, or real life experience. It might be helpful to learn from a variety of sources. Create a schedule that designates consistent blocks of time for your learning (i.e., 30 minutes a day, one morning or lunch hour a week, etc). Write down what you plan to learn and how you plan to learn it during those times.

ASSESSMENT: How will you know you learned it?

The goal of your learning is personal growth. Assess your progress by the changes you see in your thinking and your actions. If you're growing, it will become evident in your behavior. Are you able to incorporate your learning into your everyday life? Identify ways to capture your learning (in journals, file systems, online archiving) so you can access it easily when you need it.

NEXT ACTION: What will you do with what you learned?

Think about your purpose for learning. Your growth plan should include a strategy to use your learning in way that aligns with your purpose. Perhaps you will take what you are learning and teach it to someone else. Or maybe you will implement what you learned into your performance in school or on the job. Now that you've learned it, figure out how you're going to use it.

One of the best tools for establishing your personal growth plan as a consistent discipline is your calendar. This is where you'll manage your plan.

Don't make your growth plan a line item on your to-do list, make it an appointment you have each day.

INVEST YOUR TIME

The people who lead themselves well use their time wisely.

We are all given 24 hours in a day. No one gets any more or any less. The difference is how we spend that time.

Did you hear that? I used the word, "spend." We often use that word when talking about our time. This is because time is a valuable resource that we use like money. And even though we each have different amounts of money, we all have the same amount of time to spend each day.

TIME LEVELS THE PLAYING FIELD. If you can spend your time wisely, you'll make a better investment of that resource than the person who spends his or her time foolishly. Unfortunately, we don't view time as a valuable resource because we think we have so much of it. We don't think about how we spend it – until it's too late.

The downside of time is that we never get it back. I can lose or spend $20. At that point it's gone. But I can turn around and find a way to get another $20 – by working for it or borrowing it from someone else. Not so with time.

Once it's gone - it's gone.

When we truly grasp this concept, it raises our appraisal of time – from valuable resource to precious commodity.

When you lead yourself well, you make the most of your time.

The best tool I've found to manage my time is the calendar. One calendar.

Everything I do is organized around appointments. I create appointments to meet with people. I create appointments to work on projects. I create appointments to implement my growth plan. I create appointments to exercise. I create appointments to do my writing and my reading. I create appointments to give myself free time.

I don't put to-do items on my calendar. That's a different system for me. I organize my day to know how I'm basically going to use my time. I typically work hour to hour or in blocks of time. Structuring my calendar down to the minute seems a bit too tedious for me. In this way, my calendar serves as an accurate compass rather than a detailed map of my day.

Some people have multiple calendars they refer to. They have a calendar on their wall, a calendar at their office, a calendar on their phone, a calendar on their computer, and so on.

They're surrounded by all kinds of calendars.
I look at that and think to myself: *bad idea*.

Like the ring that hangs around Frodo's neck in *The Lord of the Rings*, I want one calendar to bind them, one calendar to rule them all. One calendar that is *precious*.

Personally, I use Google Calendar. You may have another calendar or calendar system you use. That's great. Let me explain why I've chosen Google Calendar. I like the way I can create different calendars to organize the various roles and responsibilities in my life. I currently have the following calendars all in one place on Google Calendar:

- Four calendars for each of my kids' events and activities
- Three calendars for work-related events and activities
- One calendar for personal events
- One calendar for birthdays (which I pull from my Facebook account)

- One calendar for special activities
- One calendar for sports team schedules (I'm a big San Francisco Giants & 49ers fan)

All of these different calendars are incorporated into ONE calendar. They're all color-coded. They're easy to look at all together or one at a time.

I like how Google Calendar integrates well with my phone or whatever screen I'm working on. I can even print it out (though I rarely do). The goal here is accessibility wherever I'm at.

Accessibility is important because you need to use and manage your calendar on a daily basis.

Create a system where you immediately put any new event or activity into your calendar. Include all of the important information and attach special notes or instructions (you can do that in Google Calendar) for you to refer back to.

I manage my calendar from three primary vantage points:

- Daily
- Weekly
- Quarterly

Daily: Establish a habit where you look at your calendar each morning and each night. Plan your day and work your plan. Incorporate blocks of time to get the projects and work done. Block out times for you to rest and nurture your soul. Time is a limited resource, but your energy is renewable. Think through your most energetic and least energetic parts of your day and plan your time accordingly. Take time to exercise. Do the things that make each day successful.

Weekly: This allows you to step back and see the rhythm of the next seven days. You can plan ahead to structure your time around the bigger events and appointments that will occur. Know what's coming. Reflect back on the previous week and see where you might need to follow up or finish up a project. Get an overall sense of your week.

Quarterly: I look at this view once or twice each month.

It is frustrating when I'm not prepared for an upcoming event or appointment. If you are working with timelines and deadlines, you will need to keep a bigger picture view, especially if you're in a leadership role. A quarterly view helps you to see where you're going. It provides a better context and sense of purpose to what you're doing on a daily and weekly basis. It's easy to find yourself living from event to event, from one deadline to the next. The quarterly view gives you a perspective beyond the daily grind.

When it comes to time, someone or something is going to spend your time if you don't take control of it.

You take responsibility for your time when you take charge of your calendar.

THE DAILY CHECK - IN

Change is necessary for improvement and growth but it doesn't happen overnight. It happens daily.

The most important appointment you have on your calendar is the one you have with yourself.

Have you ever gone for weeks, maybe even months, without seeing a friend of yours? When you finally get together, you spend the first hour of your conversation catching up, talking about all that's taken place since you last met.

The same is true with the relationship you have with yourself. If you're not taking the time to reflect on how things are going on a regular basis, you'll begin to lose sight of who you are...or worse...who you are becoming.

WHEN YOU LOSE SIGHT OF WHO YOU ARE BECOMING, YOU'LL ONLY ENGAGE IN THESE INTERNAL "CATCHING UP" CONVERSATIONS WITH YOURSELF WHEN YOU COME FACE-TO-FACE WITH A CRISIS. Instead of asking yourself what *went* wrong, isn't it better to have a regular check-in where you are able to identify what's *going* wrong?

A daily check-in is a habit of reflection and direction.

Consider it a chance to get your bearings. This is a time for you - to connect - with you.

Some people use the time to pray.
Some people use the time to center themselves.
Some people use the time to write in a journal.
Some people use the time to be silent and still.

Use the daily check-in to accomplish two things:

1. Know where you're at.
2. Know where you're headed.

You created to-do lists, timelines, and deadlines to guide you in the accomplishment of your vision and goals. The daily check-in observes where you are in the process. Do you feel like you're ahead or behind of where you want to be? Are you working on the most important matters or only the most urgent?

Next, you need to make sure you're headed in the right direction. How's your character? Are you keeping your promises? Are you motivated by the right things? Are you doing your best, working with excellence as your goal, and remaining positive?

The meeting you have with yourself each day will impact each meeting you have with others.

Leaders who lose their way are not necessarily bad people; rather, they lose their moral bearings, often yielding to seductions in their paths. Very few people go into leadership roles to cheat or do evil, yet we all have the capacity for actions we deeply regret unless we stay grounded.

The daily check-in is an investment in staying grounded.
It keeps you connected to your inner compass. It reminds you of what's most important and significant.

THE TO-DAY LIST

Most of the time, when I lay my head on the pillow at night I am tired. But before I nod off to sleep, I will have a sense of satisfaction or dissatisfaction with what was accomplished throughout the course of the day. I know if I was productive or unproductive – if I did the things that mattered or was simply busy, doing insignificant work.

I want each day to be meaningful and I want to be a good steward of the time I've been given.

When I view each day as a gift, I treat it with respect and value. I honor the time I've been given by dedicating myself to doing what matters most.

I have a short list of things that I want to try and accomplish each and every day. The list is simple and generic. **The items on the list are activities I want to habitually engage in.** They represent the best of meaningful productivity for me. It's called my ***To-Day List.***

A *To-Day* list is different than a *To-Do* list. A *To-Do* list is full of items that you may only have to do once and are tied to projects, assignments, and things that need to get done that day. A *To-Day* list contains the things I want to do EVERY DAY.

Let me show you my list. It only contains four things. But at the end of the day, if I've done these four things – I feel great!

MY TO-DAY LIST
Write something
Learn something
Lift something
Thank someone

I keep it generic because it allows me to be creative and innovative in tackling each "something/someone" throughout the day. The following is a breakdown of each action with an explanation as to why it's an important part of my list.

Write something – I want to be a better writer. I like putting my ideas and thoughts into words that others can read. Writing helps me think. It's a bit therapeutic. Plus, writing is the key to producing and providing tools and resources that others can use. I would include the design work I do in this category as well. Basically, I want to engage in the creative and creating process each day.

Learn something – I want to be a lifelong learner. I read hundreds of blogs. I read at least a book a week. I read ebooks, magazines, and listen to audio books. This is one of the main reasons I bought an iPad (it's either a good reason or a good rationalization). There are lessons to be learned everyday. Everyone has something to teach us. I want to keep my opens to opportunities for learning on a daily basis.

Lift something – I want to be physically fit. As I get older, I need to keep moving. I need to exercise. I have to be intentional about it. I use a standing desk. I take the stairs. I am a much better person, physically and mentally, if I've spent time working out. Physical fitness can be one of the hardest activities to remain consistent with. It is so easy to put it off or rationalize not doing it. Yet it pays the largest dividends in every other area of my life.

Thank someone – I want to be a grateful person. Gratitude cures many ills. I am less likely to become bitter, proud, selfish, and isolated if I take the time to thank someone every day. It's nearly impossible to have a bad attitude while expressing gratitude. One of the most powerful ways to share gratitude with others is through a handwritten note or letter.

How about you? Is there something you'd like to accomplish each and every day? Why not take the time to write out your *To-Day* list and post it somewhere as a reminder. Don't make it too difficult. I'd suggest you include no more than four or five actions on your list.

It's amazing what can happen when you identify your most significant tasks and commit to doing them every day.

ONE YEAR FROM NOW

Karen Lamb offers a motivational quote meant to inspire anyone who is interested in making the most of each day. I keep it posted on my wall (I need to make it banner size):

> "A year from now you may wish you had started today."

This speaks volumes to the inner procrastinator in me. I have to constantly tell myself, "Do It Now!" Lamb understands the difference between promises and wishes. She also knows that I wouldn't get much done if I simply waited until "I feel like it."

Lamb's quote also addresses an overwhelming fear: Could I let an entire year go by and never start the thing I know I need to start?

• Could a year go by without writing that book?

• Could a year go by without getting in the habit of exercising?

• Could a year go by without confronting an issue?

• Could a year go by without cracking open that book I need to read?

• Could a year go by without ___(fill in the blank)___?

Yes it could. Yes it has. I've even had two years go by.

I think one of the most painful of emotions is not loneliness, or the pain of failure, or even dread. It's regret.

Take your one calendar and turn back the pages to a year ago. What did you want to accomplish a year ago that remains undone? Are you better or worse?

THE SPAN OF A YEAR IS A GREAT TOOL FOR MEASURING OUR GROWTH. The question is: Can you handle what you see?

I think we often overestimate what we can accomplish in a day, a week, even a month. But there are so many challenges we could take on throughout the course of a year.

A lot can happen in a year.

- How do you measure the success or failure of your year?
- Do you look at your financial statements?
- Do you look at what the work you've done?
- Do you simply count birthdays?
- Do you rate your relationships?

You have to ask yourself the question:
Where do I want to be a year from now?

The answer may include your location, but it should be more than that. Include your dreams and your aspirations. Include the kind of habits you want to maintain and create. Tap into the opportunities to work with greater intensity in the areas of your passion and giftedness.

It could mean some sweeping changes need to occur, the kind of changes that have to happen over months and not overnight.

If the quote from Karen Lamb doesn't inspire you, perhaps your answers to the following questions will:

- Are you going to take this year more seriously than the

last one, or two, or five?

• If this were your last year on the planet, what would you want to accomplish?

• One year from now, what will you look back and hope you had started today?

TAKING RESPONSIBILITY FOR YOURSELF

In the midst of writing this book, I was watching the local news cover the resignation of one of our politicians. He'd made some obvious blunders in his personal life and he was being forced to step down. In the midst of his press conference, he made the following statement:

I accept responsibility for my actions.

As I listened and watched, I felt like it sounded a bit hollow. It didn't come across as completely sincere. I wondered what it was that left this kind of impression. Was it his body language? Was it his mannerisms? Was it the fact that he was finally coming clean about all of this now?

Then it hit me. He *accepted* responsibility...but he didn't *take* it. **There's a difference between *accepting* responsibility and *taking* responsibility.** A big difference.

Since this is a book about leading yourself well, we have to take a moment and talk about responsibility.

Specifically, the responsibility you have – to you.

You have to take responsibility. You can't simply accept responsibility. It may seem like a small, semantic nuance that sort of means the same thing. But I don't think it does.

Becoming a leader doesn't start off with the willingness to be a leader, it begins with the willingness to be responsible.

Leadership is characterized by responsibility.

When it comes to responsibility, there are often two types of consequences. The first consequence is when things go well, taking responsibility ends with praise. The second is when things go bad, taking responsibility ends with punishment.

Most people don't like punishment, but they rather enjoy praise. So they'll typically accept responsibility hoping it will end in praise and not punishment.

It is the fear of punishment that causes us to dodge responsibility for as long as we can. We cast blame on anyone and anything to get out of being punished.

Because we spend so much time and energy trying to avoid responsibility out of fear of punishment, we miss out on the reward that responsibility offers when we take it in the midst of failure and mistakes.

Take the blame. Take the consequence. Take the responsibility. Then watch what happens. **The person who immediately takes responsibility for his or her actions when things go bad earns respect.** Not only respect from others but self-respect as well.

Andrew Sullivan noted, "Errors are inevitable. The mark of character is not refusing to recognize them, but acknowledging them and taking responsibility."

Yes, there will be consequences one must face. But people admire the strength and courage of an individual who takes responsibility seriously. Taking responsibility cannot be seen as a last ditch effort because all other options have failed and one is trying to save face.

The reward of respect is given to the one who takes personal responsibility from beginning to end.

Look at some of the differences between accepting responsibility and taking responsibility.

When you accept responsibility, you're receiving it from someone else. A crisis or error occurs and people are looking for someone to be held responsible. There are a number of options, all kinds of people or processes they could lay the mantle of responsibility on for the situation. You might even try to downplay your role, offer a narrative that describes extenuating circumstances. But in the end, they point at you...and you accept it. Accepting responsibility sounds like it is one of many options.

TAKING RESPONSIBILITY IS MUCH MORE AGGRESSIVE. When you take responsibility, you own it. When you take it, you invest yourself in it. Whatever the outcome, the responsibility is yours. It always has been. No questions asked. You take it.

The difference between accepting and taking is important when it focuses on you being responsible for you. People tend to accept responsibility for their actions after they've been caught. If you watch enough television you can see the pattern.

1. Accusation.
2. Deny, deny, deny, deny.
3. Proven beyond a shadow of a doubt that you're guilty.
4. Blame, blame, blame.
5. The hammer is going to fall hard on you.
6. Accept responsibility.

Taking responsibility separates itself from accepting responsibility in one very clear way.

The person who takes responsibility will do so for both the decision and consequence.

From beginning to end. No blaming. No pointing fingers elsewhere. I take it. It's mine. Good or bad. I own it all. That's different than accepting responsibility. Accepting responsibility sounds like I'm now willing to place the responsibility on myself from this point forward.

On a side note, accepting responsibility may be appropriate when it involves your influence in the growth of others.

You're a parent and your kid screwed up. You accept responsibility for not raising them properly.

You're a coach and your player didn't perform well. You accept responsibility for not preparing them appropriately.

You're a teacher and your student fails a test. You accept responsibility for not instructing them adequately.

In each of these situations, you are in a position of influence and authority. This means you hold some level of responsibility. But your goal, in each of these instances, is for the kid, the player, or the student to take responsibility for themselves. Sooner or later, they have to stop blaming their parents, their coaches, and their teachers for the bad decisions and the consequences that occur.

RESPONSIBILITY (PART 2)

Taking responsibility is a sign of maturity. Have you ever seen little children get caught doing something they are well aware they shouldn't be doing? Their responses are typical.

What are you doing? *Nothing.*
Who took the last cookie? *It wasn't me.*
Why is your little sister crying? *I didn't do it.*

From an early age our innate, first response is denial... then blame (people or circumstance) ...then admit...then accept.

Those who lead themselves well understand their first response to their own mistake or error is responsibility.

Winston Churchill said, *"Responsibility is the price for greatness."* The moment that your failure comes to light, you have a choice to make. You can move in the direction of *excellence* or *excuses*. Of course, the immediate temptation you will face when you're found out is toward excuses.

But I have just had so much homework...

I assigned this to someone else and they haven't come through...

I called and left a message but no one got back to me...

It's not my fault...

The thing is, every one of those statements may be TRUE. Yet when they're spoken in the context of unfulfilled responsibilities, they ring hollow and sound only like excuses.

You will move toward excellence when you take responsibility and respond with something like...

I dropped the ball. I will get right on it...

I am sorry that I completely missed that. It's my own fault...

I will find a way to make that happen today...

With statements like that, people are more willing to move past the mistake and get back to work. When you take responsibility and work to make things right, it makes things better.

It's what occurs in RESPONSE to those down times that will define your direction toward excuses or excellence.

With *excuses*, I'm thinking of things like: blame, pride, continually making the same mistake, defensive, insensitive, dogmatic, and being a victim.

With *excellence*, I recognize it in things like: apologies, humility, learn from mistakes, flexibility, solving problems, intentional, and owning it.

When it comes to taking responsibility, you can offer excuses or excellence ...the choice is yours.

THE CORPORATION OF YOU

Imagine for a moment that you are the CEO of a small corporation. In fact, it's a very small corporation. You aren't just the CEO, you're also the Chairman of the Board, the President, and the only employee the corporation has. You are in charge.

Your corporation exists to serve the needs of one client: you. Yup, you're in charge of the Corporation of You.

As the CEO, you must ensure that your corporation meets the needs of your one and only client. You must make sure that your sole stockholder in the company (you) sees a return on investment. You make decisions every day as to the viability or liability of your corporation.

You see, the only way your corporation grows is if your client grows (you). So you need to get to know all there is to know about your client. That way you can better meet your client's needs and know where to encourage your client's growth.

It would be helpful for the corporation to sit down with

your client and map out a plan that would be mutually beneficial to both the client and the corporation.

When it comes to the Corporation of You, if you grow the client, you grow the corporation.

There might be times when your client pushes back a little bit and tries to resist the services of the corporation. You must be mindful of this and refer the client back to the plan and to the rationale behind the plan. The client wants the corporation to succeed just as much as you do. But it's easy to get sidetracked by other corporations who are vying for your client's interests.

There's the *Corporation of Convenience*. This very lazy organization works hard to make everything easy for the client. This corporation attempts to encourage the client to avoid anything slightly difficult or painful.

Then there's the *Corporation of Someone Else*. This corporation will try to turn your client into someone he or she isn't.

The *Corporation of Someday* is sneaky. It will lay out a great plan that it never quite gets around to implementing for its client.

Also, there's the *Corporation of Almost*. An offshoot of the Someday people, it is great at starting something for its client but somehow derails their client, causing him or her to never finish what was started.

Finally, there's the *Corporation of Stuck*. They have an excellent track record of protecting their client from change or growth. They work hard to keep everything the same, day in and day out.

At any point in time, one of these corporations is vying for a takeover. It happens. I've seen the Corporation of You start to adopt the business model of one of these other corporations. Soon you're ripe for the picking. If one of these corporations stages a takeover and succeeds, they will end up absorbing the Corporation of You into their own enterprise.

The good news is the Corporation of You is on the brink of a bull market. Investor confidence is high and you have an opportunity here to show signs of gradual, yet marked improvement and an increase in future potential.

As the CEO of the Corporation of You, it's probably time to hold another stakeholders meeting with your client and offer a State of the Corporation address to see where you're at. If you're truly honest with your client, you'll be able to overcome the weaknesses of the corporation while capitalizing on the corporation's strengths.

Once you have an authentic view of where you are, it's a lot easier to plot the course for the future.

YOU'RE NOT A MONK

Okay, you might be a monk. But statistics will probably prove out that there will only be about seven monks who read this. Chances are good, you're not a monk. But even if you are one...this will be beneficial to you.

You are responsible for your own growth. You are the CEO of the Corporation of You. Self-leadership means you are the one who is leading, and the person you're leading is you.

BUT YOU DON'T HAVE TO GO IT ALONE. Even monks work in community.

Think of it this way - even CEOs need advisors. A board of directors. If you lead yourself in isolation you are actually limiting yourself.

If you're the only voice that speaks into your leadership development...
- then it's all based on your IQ.
- then it's all flowing out of your own, somewhat limited, experience.

- then it's all conceived on your sole, maybe narrow, perspective.
- then it's all paid for out of your resources.

Do you see how limiting that can be?

YOU ARE RESPONSIBLE FOR YOUR OWN GROWTH. But you don't have to be the only resource for your own growth. Get some other folks involved in the process. Just make sure they're the right folks.

What I'm talking about here is accountability.

There are two kinds of accountability. There's the kind where people are checking in on you to make sure you're not putting yourself in danger. Then there's the kind where people are checking in on you to make sure you are making yourself into a better person.

When people hear the word accountability – they typically think of the first kind. They don't want a group of people looking over their shoulder trying to point out all of the bad things.

But not very many leaders pull a group of people

together for the other kind of accountability. The kind where people sit around the table and make sure you are leading yourself well. They're purpose is to grow you, not to ground you.

Of course, if you truly create a group of people who will focus on the second kind of accountability, they will probably have to address some of the first kind as well.

WE ALL HAVE BLINDSPOTS. We all operate out of a limited perspective. If you've put together a group of people you can trust, wouldn't you want to hear how they see things? Especially if they don't see things the way you see things?

In this way, accountability isn't just a rubber stamp. It's not a bunch of people who, while you sit in the center, sit in a circle telling you how wonderful you are. They are a group of people who are interested in your growth.

And based on that priority, they're going to ask you questions that may sting a little bit. They're going to make observations that point out some of your lesser qualities. They're going to ask you to be truthful about your motives, your rationalizations, and your actions.

There are two primary qualifications for a person to serve in a group like that for you:

1. You trust them.

2. They want what's best for you.

If you can't trust them, then you won't be completely honest with them.

If they don't want what's best for you, then you can't trust them.

I know I keep saying group. I think you need more than one other person. But they don't have to all show up at the same time in a meeting of the Corporation of You Roundtable. You can meet with these folks individually if you like. You can rely on them for different areas of your life.

What you're looking for is perspective, and help, and feedback, and support, and growth.

The reality is you cannot stay grounded by yourself.
Leaders depend on people closest to them to stay centered. You should seek out people who influence you

in profound ways and stay connected to them. Look for people who know you best. People who aren't impressed by titles, prestige, or how much money you have; instead, they worry that these outward symbols may be causing a loss of authenticity within you.

Take a moment and write down the names of three or four people that you can approach. You want to ask them to help you lead yourself well. You want their honest feedback and their candid opinions. You want to hear their perspective. You want them to speak into your life because you believe that will help you to be a better person.

Work out the details with them. They'll want to know how much time and energy this may take. All I can say is...it depends.

What I do know is if, 1. You trust them and, 2. They want what's best for you, you'll work something out.

One more thing for the monks in the reading audience (or if you're considering becoming a monk). The image of a monk is often one of isolation in a wilderness setting. But most monastic societies are set up as vibrant, working communities. In fact, monks keep each other accountable to the vows they have taken.

Thus, those who enter the monastic life have a greater circle of accountability than most any of us do.

NO SHORTCUTS TO
GOOD CHARACTER

A person can be a leader without good character. But not for very long.

One of the most important reasons you need to lead yourself first before you lead others is to develop your character. **Your character is the combination of all of the decisions, both big and small, you've made.** They come together to form who you are on the inside. Your character is strengthened when you keep your promises. When you are the same person in public that you are in private. When your words and your actions agree.

IT TAKES TIME TO BUILD YOUR CHARACTER. It's a track record of what you say you're going to do and what you've done. It is a long, slow process of building trust with people. Over time, people get to know who you are... really.

You can try to hide your true character from people. You can put on an act. You might even fool them for a little while. But over time, your authentic self comes through.

If you've done the right things in public and private, you will slowly build a strong character. Character grows like an oak tree. A person's reputation grows like a weed.

But for all the time and energy it takes to develop good character, to become a person that people trust because of what they see on the outside and sense on the inside – it can be lost in a moment. One bad decision, one fateful mistake and your character is shattered.

THAT'S WHY THERE ARE NO SHORTCUTS TO GOOD CHARACTER. You can't buy good character and you can't borrow someone else's good character. Your character must be forged through your own experiences and the choices you make during those experiences.

When life is going well and everyone is happy, we don't think too much about character. Character doesn't seem all that important when the team is winning and everyone is getting paid and getting along. But when a crisis shows up, we start to find out what you're made of.

Crisis and conflict do two things to character:

1. They expose your character for what it really is.
2. They provide an opportunity to grow good character.

When a conflict occurs, people are watching how you're going to react. They want to see if you're the same person in times of trouble as you are in times of ease. They're watching your attitude and your approach to the situation. If you remain consistent, they can see that there's something inside of you that keeps you grounded when others are losing their heads.

But conflict also has a way of growing good character. Conflict is difficult. If you can make it through the conflict with your character intact, the experience will make you stronger. You'll have more resolve to stay true to your convictions and make good choices during the difficulties.

Think of the formation of your character like a sculptor chiseling away at a block of marble. Each decision you make shapes the person you are becoming. For good or for bad, you are building up or tearing down your character.

Your character is your responsibility.

You can't blame someone else for your bad character or give credit to another if you have good character. It is yours and yours alone.

Once you have begun to establish good character, it will affect the way people respond to you. They will know what kind of person you are. They'll know that you won't want to be a part of anything that would damage your character. They will give you the benefit of the doubt if someone tries to malign your character. You'll be known for what you will or won't do.

And all of this leads to trust. **When you have good character, people know they can trust you.** They can trust you with their money, with their time, with their skills, with their relationships, and so on. The track record you develop through your good character is a powerful influence.

John Wooden, famous UCLA basketball coach, stated, "*Ability may get you to the top, but it takes character to keep you there.*" Think about how many people you've seen rise to a position of leadership. They were qualified and skilled and from all accounts, perfect for the job. But soon, there were questions, rumors, and murmurs that something wasn't quite right. Until one day, it came out into the open - the leader had an affair, or broke a promise, or stole some money, or cheated on taxes, or made a horrible decision. And in a moment's time, trust was gone because the person's true character was revealed.

Unfortunately, these stories happen way too often. People are placed into positions because of their capabilities. But they don't possess the level of their character necessary to succeed in the position. Inevitably, crisis and conflict will occur - and the person doesn't possess the character to work through it.

Capabilities without character are a train wreck waiting to happen.

Here are some immediate steps you can take to develop good character.

1. Make decisions based on your values and not on the circumstances.

2. Be consistent.

3. Reflect on decisions and experiences. Learn from them. Don't repeat the same mistake twice.

4. Be humble and teachable.

5. Only engage in actions that align with your values. Don't settle for less than your best or think you'll try to get away with something "just this one time."

Take a moment to reflect on the following character assessment (10 qualities that demonstrate good character). Rate yourself on a scale of 1-10, with 1 being poor and 10 being excellent.

1. Live by the same standards you hold others to.

    1   2   3   4   5   6   7   8   9   10

2. Be the same person in public you are in private.

    1   2   3   4   5   6   7   8   9   10

3. Your words and your actions agree.

    1   2   3   4   5   6   7   8   9   10

4. Don't shy away from hard work.

    1   2   3   4   5   6   7   8   9   10

5. Keep your promises.

    1   2   3   4   5   6   7   8   9   10

6. Associate with others of high character.

    1   2   3   4   5   6   7   8   9   10

7. Follow through on responsibilities.

    1   2   3   4   5   6   7   8   9   10

8. Don't participate in behavior that puts the rest of your team in jeopardy.

    1   2   3   4   5   6   7   8   9   10

9. Maintain your integrity and maturity in difficult situations.

    1   2   3   4   5   6   7   8   9   10

10. Put the needs of others before your own.

    1   2   3   4   5   6   7   8   9   10

Protect your character. Know where you're most susceptible. Address your weak areas.

STRETCH YOURSELF – THE LAW OF THE RUBBER BAND

We live in a society that works hard to avoid discomfort.

Throughout the course of any given day, we navigate towards comfortable instead of doing what's necessary to work through uncomfortable.

When we attempt to sidestep this process, you and I miss out on a special reward. There is a prize that awaits each of us on the other side of difficult effort.

THE PRIZE IS CALLED GROWTH. But growth doesn't come automatically and it doesn't come easy. Growth requires change. Change is often uncomfortable. But just because it's uncomfortable doesn't mean it's bad. Why have we taught ourselves that discomfort or pain is always bad? In many instances, it can be very good.

Think about the process of growing your muscles. The physiological process sounds horrifying. In order to get stronger, you need to tear your muscle tissue. You need to lift a heavy enough weight that you're uncomfortable (think pain, soreness, fatigue, raw exertion).

Once you've endured the uncomfortable process, you allow your muscles time to recover and heal. It's in that process they get bigger and stronger.

The science behind muscle growth is fascinating. Research has shown that in order to increase muscle mass, stress must be put on the body, leading to increased hormone release, and increased flow of nutrients into the muscle, and with rest, muscles will grow.

The muscle building process is the same in nature. In scientific terms, the muscle building process is called "hypertrophy".

When you visit the gym, you put your muscles under stress by lifting weights. Your muscles come closer to failure with every repetition that you do, which means at one point, they will "give out" and you will not be able to do any more reps, no matter how hard you push yourself.

As your muscle approaches failure, these reps create deeper and deeper inroads through the muscle fiber, resulting in what we call "micro-tears".

Basically, what you are doing is breaking down your muscle fibers by causing actual damage to the muscle. Your body reacts to this damage by repairing the muscles.

THE MUSCLE REPAIR PROCESS IS THE KEY PART IN BUILDING MUSCLE. Your body begins repairing muscle tissue when you stop putting stress on your muscles, in other words after stopping your workout.

The thing is, your body sees the damage to your muscles as a threat to its survival, so it will rebuild the damaged muscle tissue bigger and stronger than before to protect against future threats.

So this increased muscle size and strength is a natural evolutionary response to the micro-tears that your muscles have suffered due to the heavy weight training you performed. It's as simple as that.

But it's not that simple. If growth were easy, everyone would do it.

Recently, my son turned eighteen. He proudly announced

that he was an adult now. I smiled and acknowledged that by law, he was a legal adult.

Then I added, "but maturity doesn't come with birthdays."

When it comes to growth you need to follow the Law Of The Rubber Band. This law states:

You will be most useful when you're being stretched.

Think about it. A rubber band, flimsily draped around some objects, doesn't do a bit of good. It's only when the rubber band is stretched and tightly wound around something that it's most useful.

The Law of the Rubber Band encourages you to work through uncomfortable rather than always trying to find comfortable. It is a reminder that you cannot become the person you are meant to be by remaining the person that you are. You continually need to be stretched (not to the point of snapping) in order to continue to grow and develop.

THE LAW OF THE RUBBER BAND REMINDS ME THERE IS A REWARD ON THE FAR SIDE OF UNCOMFORTABLE. There is a comfort that can only be achieved by working through uncomfortable instead of avoiding it. It expands my comfort zone.

It's about development, not destruction. If you push your muscles too hard, you'll do serious damage. You must find the balance. A properly stretched rubber band is useful. If you pull a rubber band too hard, it will break, rendering it useless.

It's also about potential and capacity. You'll never know what you're capable of until you push yourself past your (often self-imposed) limits. Being stretched involves risk, it involves discipline, and it takes a lot of courage.

THE SHAPE OF EXERCISE

Now it's time to get really personal. I want to talk to you about your physical fitness. You knew it was coming. Didn't you?

I've got one question: *Are you in shape?*

If you're anything like me, you're never really satisfied with where you're at physically.

I'm amazed at how many people who lead others don't do what it takes to lead themselves well in this area. The reasons are similar in most cases:

1. I'm too busy.
2. I'm too tired.
3. I'll get to it later.

We have an obesity problem in America. It stems from eating too much and moving too little.

I know it's important to get your mind right, to develop good character, and to keep your promises.

Unfortunately, too many leaders make excuses for their level of physical fitness. They have compartmentalized their physical health from other areas. They haven't made the connection – that engaging in the disciplined rigor of maintaining one's physical health leads to improvements and growth in all other areas of life.

One of the most practical and beneficial ways you can lead yourself first is to be physically fit.

- You feel better about the way you look.
- You have more energy.
- You have a clearer mind.
- You sleep better.
- You feel better.

It has a dramatic effect on your perspective and outlook.

I learned this lesson in life later than I should have. In the summer of 2010 I was finally fed up. I was the biggest I had ever been and I felt like I was one cheeseburger away from a heart attack.

After doing a little research and relying on the

recommendation of a couple of my friends, I started a program called P90X.

I stuck with it. I pushed through it. I rearranged my schedule to complete it each day. I made a promise to do it and I kept that promise. At the end of the 90 days (yes, that's 90 days in a row) I was a different person.

You don't transform your body in a day (it took you more than a day to get where you are). But you can change your body a little bit each day if you're dedicated to it on a daily basis.

I think exercise is one of the easiest things for a leader to rationalize not doing.

When a person does the work of character building or learning from their experiences, they can do that from the comfort of their office or workplace.

Exercise often requires a change of scenery. It requires a change of clothes. And if you're doing it right, it requires you to sweat.

Exercise fits well with the previous discussion about

comfort and discomfort (we feel like a stiff rope rather than a rubber band). Getting started in an exercise program is one of the most uncomfortable things you can do. You have to work through all of that initial soreness. You are completely out of breath after two minutes of cardio. You feel like you're going to die.

People stop working out and exercising after two days because it hurts too much. They're not willing to push through the initial discomfort to begin the process of retraining and reshaping their bodies.

But there are two types of pain at work here:

Bad pain is the result of you being out of shape and having a sore back because you're belly's too big. **Good pain** is the result of working to get in shape and having a sore back because you were recently introduced to free weights.

There are some things a leader can hide (at least for awhile). You can hide your true feelings. You can hide your intentions and your motives.

BUT YOU CAN'T HIDE YOUR PHYSICAL FITNESS. You see

yourself in the mirror. You know how you feel after you walk (or crawl) up a flight of stairs.

And you know, deep down, that you need to do something about it before you experience a crisis of some kind.

I'm not advocating that you get supermodel thin or starve yourself. I'm encouraging you to improve your overall fitness and to invest time exercising on a daily basis. Yes... every day. It's that important.

You will improve your confidence.
You will improve your health.
You will improve your discipline.
You will improve.

WAYS I GET IN MY OWN WAY

I think we need to take a break for a moment and get honest. At least, let me get honest and you just listen in.

I don't want you to get the wrong idea about this book. I didn't write this thing as some sort of "I've-got-it-all-figured-out-and-now-I'm-going-to-tell-you-how" manual. I'm no expert. Just observant. And learning.

There's a thought that crosses my mind after I get all excited, motivated, and inspired to do the right thing. It hits me like a sledgehammer to the side of the head. It's the realization that I'm not that good. When this moment comes, I have a choice to make. I can use it to move forward with humility or I can allow it to create some type of self-loathing cycle that keeps me trapped in the same old habits.

I vote for humility. But humility only comes through honestly and openly acknowledging all of the ways I haven't led myself well up to this point. I need to confess it. Take responsibility for it. Learn from it. Then move forward.

With that in mind, I thought I'd dig down deep into the archives of my personal experience. I want to share some of the ways (I know there's a lot more) that I have missed the mark for no other reason than...me. I was leading myself well – growing and learning. Then suddenly I ran into a wall of my own making.

I wrote this section to show you that I'm guilty of some of the very things I'm encouraging you to not do.

Self-leadership is a growth process. More often than not, I'm the person who gets in the way of that process. I tend to be my biggest obstacle.

The good news is I've learned something from each of following, self-inflicted actions. I've started to look at myself first when I feel stuck. I figure out what I need to change because I'm typically the one who needs to do the right thing, to get out of my own way so I can move forward.

Here's my list. Perhaps you'll see yourself in one or two of these.

1. I don't do anything. I hope there will be some cosmic force that causes things to work out on their own.

2. I wait for just the right moment. To me, the right moment is a combination of feelings, environmental conditions, and personal mojo. Unfortunately, it rarely arrives.

3. I don't really want to change in order to grow. I'd rather just read, write, think about, reflect on, and even analyze it instead of doing the hard work of actually changing.

4. I'm not flexible enough. This is probably true both physically (I need to stretch more) and mentally (I need to stretch more).

5. I'm not accountable. It's funny how the need for independence can quickly lead to isolation.

6. My inner dialogue isn't helping. Thinking about how many statements in my head start with: "but...", "I can't...", "if only...", and "wait...".

7. I don't have a clear picture of what I want or need to do. And if that picture is blurry, then my day-to-day tasks will be fuzzy as well.

8. I'm unmotivated. This means I've lost touch with things like passion, meaning, purpose, and significance. It also stems from becoming a bit too self-centered.

9. I'm undisciplined. The inner slacker finds a way to do anything but the thing I need to be doing.

10. I want it now. And if I can't have it now, I'm not willing to walk through the process to arrive or achieve or accomplish it later.

11. I work toward comfortable instead of working through uncomfortable.

12. I don't finish. Truth is, if I don't finish then starting doesn't count.

13. I compare. I compare the best in others to the worst in me and I always come up short.

Are you depressed yet? I know I am. I don't want to be the person described in this list. I hope you don't want to be that kind of person either.

In the process of leading yourself well, it's important to

stop and acknowledge (confess) that you've blown it. Take responsibility for it. Learn the lessons that each failure has within it. And move forward.

I encourage you to create your own list. Identify where you are failing or floundering when it comes to leading yourself well.

Whether you are looking at your own list or reading through mine, ask yourself, *"What would the opposite of this be?"*

Then do that. That's what I'm working on.

LEARNING FROM MY MISTAKES

Leading yourself well is a process of learning what works and what doesn't.

You want to do more of what works and less of what doesn't.

Sometimes, you discover what works by trying something until it doesn't work. We call these things mistakes (sometimes it's called failure). When it comes to mistakes, it's not a matter of if they'll occur; it's only a matter of when (if you're growing).

Your perspective on mistakes will determine how you handle mistakes. If you view mistakes as something to always be avoided, you will shy away from situations and responsibilities where mistakes may occur.

But, if you are willing to see mistakes as the unavoidable step toward growth and success, you will look for opportunities to work and lead in areas of innovation, creativity, and intentional risk.

"The job of leadership is not to avoid failure but to help the team succeed in spite of it." - Author Unknown

LEADING YOURSELF WELL INVOLVES YOUR REACTION AND RESPONSE TO YOUR MISTAKES. The leader's first response to mistakes is responsibility. The second response is to figure out what you can learn.

I am fortunate to work in a place that encourages me to try and helps me to learn when my attempts don't work as expected. Some work environments don't want people to make mistakes, don't want people to talk about making mistakes, and punish people when mistakes occur. I'm not talking about mistakes in the area of moral failure or failure with extreme consequences. I'm talking about the kind of mistakes that naturally occur as a result of healthy risk and innovation.

Here is my perspective on making a mistake: **I'm not afraid of it. I don't want to repeat it. I do want to learn from it. I am better from the experience. I'm not afraid of failing in the future.**

The Rhodium Rule applies well here. A healthy perspective on my own mistakes will inspire a healthy perspective in others. When I identify my mistakes as learning experiences, it frees others to look at their own mistakes in a similar light. It's contagious.

Instead of decreasing morale, a healthy perspective on mistakes can increase momentum. There's more energy to try again, to find a better way, to take what I've learned and not simply know it, but implement it and share it. Some people call this process striving for excellence.

When you have a healthy perspective and learn from your mistakes and failures, you aren't in danger of becoming a failure. *Isn't this typically our greatest fear when it comes to making a mistake or failing?*

Some of your best learning will come in the moments when plans don't pan out, hopes don't happen, and your best guess was the wrong one.

Mistakes and failure, often seen as a weakness, can enhance your strengths if handled properly.

An unhealthy perspective results in a paralyzing fear of

making mistakes. When this happens you run the risk of experiencing the following negative side effects:

Self-pity – You feel sorry for yourself. As time goes on you take less responsibility for your inactivity and start thinking of yourself as a victim.

Excuses – You can fall down many times, but you won't be a failure until you say that somebody pushed you. In fact, when you make a mistake and then offer an excuse for it you add a second mistake to your first. You can break out of the fear cycle only by taking personal responsibility for your actions or inaction.

Misused Energy – Constant fear divides the mind and causes you to lose focus. If you are going in too many directions at once, you won't get anywhere. It's comparable to stomping on the gas pedal of a car that's in neutral.

Hopelessness – Continual fear and inaction will rob you of hope. Henry Wadsworth Longfellow described the situation in this way: "The setting of a great hope is like the setting of the sun. The brightness of our life is gone."

I'm not encouraging you to make mistakes on purpose. It will happen if you're truly growing and improving. And when it happens, remember the wise words of Mahatma Ghandi, "My imperfections and failures are as much a blessing from God as my successes and my talents and I lay them both at his feet."

HOW DO YOU TALK
TO YOURSELF?

As you're reading this book, you're having a conversation. It's not one that those around you can hear. It's inside your head. Yup...you hear the voices too don't you?

You see, you're having a conversation with me as you read. You're agreeing, arguing, pushing back, and responding to what I've written here. I'm not there with you now. But because you're reading my words, and my thoughts, we're engaged in a type of conversation.

But you're also talking to yourself. You're own voice is the most familiar voice in your head. You constantly see the world through your own thinking. You are in a constant conversation with you.

When you begin to think about how to lead yourself well, you have to consider how you talk to yourself. What kinds of conversations are going on inside your head?

MOST OF OUR ACTIONS STARTED OFF AS THOUGHTS. Thoughts that came about in the midst of the ongoing conversation. They started in our heads before they played themselves out in our hands and feet and mouth.

For many of us, we can't begin to talk about modifying our behaviors until we deal with the conversation going on inside our mind. You and I need to evaluate the way we talk to ourselves. Sounds crazy, huh?

A title or position doesn't make you a leader. A leader emerges when a person begins to lead someone or something.

In order to do what a leader does, a person must first begin to think like a leader thinks.

Leadership actions are preceded by leadership thoughts.

In other words, certain thoughts inspire certain behaviors.

Think about how important having confidence is. Confidence is a belief that you can do it. That you're capable. Confidence is the ability to doubt your doubts, knowing you have what it takes to do what needs to be done. Confidence is a thought before it's displayed through your actions.

If you lack confidence, it's because you've allowed something (or someone) to change your thinking. Some circumstance or outcome or crisis or comment has caused the voice in your head to say, "You can't do it." And not only does the voice in your head speak...but you choose to listen and act accordingly.

It's important to evaluate what you're saying to yourself. I can't stress this enough. Unfortunately, the voice in your head isn't always looking out for your best interests.

For example, let's say you've made a promise to yourself that you're going to exercise every day. You've created an appointment and that appointment starts in five minutes. All of a sudden, the voice in your head starts in: "you're too busy", "you're too tired", "you have more important things to do", "this is going to be uncomfortable and the couch is more comfortable", and so on.

Can you believe it?!? The voice in your head is LYING to you. And you realize (in some strange, schizophrenic kind of way) that the other voice in the conversation is YOU. Time to take control of the conversation?

You can overcome the voice of resistance by choosing to act in spite of the voice.

Appropriate action quiets the voice.

You can choose to ignore the voice by listening to other voices. I like to listen to podcasts, read good books, and listen to trusted friends.

You can recognize the voice for what it is - a lie that doesn't have your best interest at heart.

When I started writing this book, I heard the voice loudly in my head: *"Who are you to write something about self-leadership?"*, and *"You don't have time to write"*, and *"Who is going to read a word of what you have to say?"*

You know what I did. I sat down and started writing. As I wrote, the voice – the inner conversation began to change. In the act of typing the words, my focus changed. Instead of having a conversation about why I can't, I slowly began to talk to myself about why I can.

- I didn't care if I failed. *I had to try.*

- I didn't worry about what people thought. *I wanted to share what I thought and believed.*

- I got honest about my motives for doing this. *I wanted to help others be better leaders by learning what it means to lead themselves first.*

If you don't fight and wrestle with the voice that tells you why you can't, you'll never understand all of the deeper reasons of why you can.

Your best work occurs when you've done the hard work of changing the conversation in your head. When you choose to not listen to the voice when it offers excuses.

You know you're heading in the right direction when you can honestly analyze your inner dialogue and recognize when the voice is holding you back.

STRENGTHS AND WEAKNESSES

You have strengths and weaknesses. We know this is true because every job interview you'll ever go to will ask you to describe them.

There's a growing movement to encourage leaders to work within their area of strength and delegate to their area of weakness. This is pretty good advice. You can't be great at everything. There will be certain tasks you do better than other tasks. But I don't hear much conversation about those areas where a leader can never, ever be weak.

When it comes to leading yourself first, we need to have this conversation.

Your character must always be a strength. If it becomes a weakness you're in trouble. You can't delegate your character development to someone else. It's your job. Every time. Every day.

YOUR INTEGRITY IS NOT A PERSONALITY TRAIT. Therefore you can't claim you don't have it on a certain test.

In fact, each day of your life is a test to see if you can maintain your integrity or not.

YOUR ATTITUDE IS NOT AN APTITUDE. You either choose to have a positive one or you don't. You can't claim you haven't been properly trained.

You can claim you're not skilled at accounting or athletics, but you can't write "susceptible to temper tantrums and holding grudges" on your application.

When it comes to the discussion about strengths and weaknesses, be mindful of those things that must always be strengths and can never be weaknesses.

Lousy character and no integrity and a bad attitude and anger issues, etc – are not weaknesses. We call those flaws.

There's a difference.

If you have a weakness in your skill set, we can delegate that area or train you to some level of competence. But we can't cover over your flaws. You need to fix those. You can try to hide them. But at some point, the truth will come out. Do you understand the difference between a flaw and a weakness?

A weakness leads to poor results.
A flaw leads to poor character.

A weakness can be improved over time.
A flaw needs to be fixed and dealt with immediately.

A weakness is a production issue.
A flaw is a person-hood issue.

A weakness can be tolerated because we can find someone with complementary strengths.
A flaw can never be tolerated.

A person with a weakness can be moved around to a more suitable area of the organization that better suits his or her strengths.

A person with a flaw is detrimental to any area of the organization until the flaw is dealt with and removed.

You won't be good at everything – that's why there's the

strengths and weaknesses question. But you must always be good at things like character, integrity, and attitude - there's no grey area.

You can acknowledge your weaknesses, but you must take responsibility for your flaws.

You can be successful as a leader even with your weaknesses. You will suffer as a leader if you don't fix your flaws.

THE POWER OF EXAMPLE

If you want to be a leader, you will need to learn to communicate in such a way that people are inspired and find the motivation to do the right thing.

The best leaders often do that without ever saying a word.

If people watched a video of your life today with the volume "muted" what would they learn about you?

One of the most powerful ways you can communicate those types of messages is through your example. This is motivation behind the Rhodium Rule.

Do unto yourself what will inspire the best in others.

Are you starting to understand the power of leading yourself well? It is one of the most influential practices you can perform as a leader. Of course, you don't lead yourself well simply to influence others. But then again, you do.

You offer your best as one of the primary means of inspiring the best in others.

People do what people see. It's a familiar axiom.

PEOPLE ARE INSPIRED BY THE ACTIONS OF THEIR LEADERS MORE SO THAN THE WORDS OF THEIR LEADERS. While I'm not advocating for silent leadership, I am promoting leadership that goes first. Leaders that set the tone with their own lives before asking others to set the tone with theirs.

I wrote this book because I want to raise up a generation of leaders worth imitating. Leaders who aren't perfect. Leaders who make mistakes. Leaders who may not always have the right answer. Leaders who are honest about their struggles. Yet, every step of the way, we are encouraged by their example of character, integrity, and personal responsibility. Not only do we want to be like them, we want to work closely with them. We want to follow them.

I have served under leaders who have proven to be good examples of what not to do. Their daily habits, personal values, and observable behavior stood in stark contrast to the kind of person I wanted to be. As I watched them and learned what not to do, there was a gnawing realization...

I will always be an example to someone else. The question is: What kind of example will I be?

Let's take one's ability to be a good example a step further. I think each of us has the ability to be a good example for a day...for a week. For an extended period of time while everything is going well. But when crisis hits, when circumstances don't line up in our favor, that's when our true example shows through.

That's why your example, as a leader, will always flow out of who you are. *Who* you are as a person will influence *what* you do as a person. You must become the right kind of person in order to do the right kinds of things on a regular and consistent basis.

You can fake it for only so long.

Authenticity has a way of showing up when we least expect it.

Leadership starts with you because your example is one of

your most meaningful and lasting forms of influence.

- You work hard to inspire others to work hard.
- You are honest to inspire others to be honest.
- You take responsibility to inspire others to take responsibility.

One of the most eye-opening moments in my life came from my son. I saw him doing something that he knew he shouldn't be doing. When I confronted him on it, he said these words...

But you do it Dad.

All he was doing was following my example. There were all kinds of ways I could have rationalized, or explained, or deflected his comment away.

But all I could do is look him in the eye, take responsibility, and tell him, "You're right and I shouldn't do that."

People are going to watch how you lead yourself and make a decision whether or not they are going to let you lead them.

It all comes down to the example you set on a daily basis. Are you setting the kind of example that inspires others to be their best? Or are you setting the kind of example that others want to avoid in their own lives?

HONE YOUR HUMILITY

Great leaders are better defined by such traits as integrity, determination, and strength of character, then by stage presence and strength of personality.

You aren't going to get it perfect every time. In fact you probably won't get it perfect most of the time. Perfection is a pipe dream. Excellence is the goal. And a lack of excellence is merely an excuse.

But how do you handle the missteps, the mistakes, and the mishaps (your fault or someone else's)?

With humility.

Humility is something you work toward but never really achieve. It seems the minute you think or know you're humble...you're no longer humble.

Humility is the ability to recognize that the world is bigger than just you.

It is a perspective you carry around with you. It

acknowledges the work, sacrifice, and service of others. It knows that anything you accomplish on your own... didn't happen on your own. Humility softens your edges. You can be ambitious and still be humble. You can be a leader and still be humble. You can be decisive and still be humble.

You're easier to relate to when you're humble. You're easier to be around.

One of the best motivations to be humble is realizing when you're the opposite: proud or boastful or egotistical. You find yourself looking at the world through the lens of "it's all about me." It is an inner arrogance that others can sense.

Humility encourages you to live in a paradox. On one hand, leadership starts with you. You must lead yourself well. Part of your focus, attention, and energy is on you.

But it can't be all about you.

When you act with humility, you don't force your way in the world. You allow your example to speak more loudly than your words.

You are mindful that those around you are living out their own story, in their own way. You influence more than you demand.

HUMILITY ISN'T SYNONYMOUS WITH WEAKNESS. In many instances, the humble leader will operate out of a strong sense of character, purpose, and values. Humility moves the energy away from attempts to stroke our own ego.

Humility is having a realistic and authentic view of ourselves. When we lack humility, we think more highly of ourselves than we ought. We think we're bigger than we are. We move ourselves into the center of the story.

One of the ways you can develop a humble spirit is to act in humble ways without claiming to be humble. No one can make you humble. It only grows and develops in your response to the difficult situations. The moment you claim humility, you lose it. Humility is a quiet and secretive journey that slowly displays itself in your life over time.

Watch what happens when you act in these ways:

1. Serve your enemies.
2. Treat others better than they treat you or they treat

themselves.

3. Admit and acknowledge your weaknesses while contributing in the area of your strengths.

4. Be grateful. Express it every time you feel it.

5. Encourage others through praise and empower others with the spotlight.

6. Ask more questions. Offer less answers.

7. Honor people and appreciate any honor given to you.

8. Talk about others more. Talk about yourself less.

HUMILITY RECOGNIZES THE INTERDEPENDENCE OF THINGS. If anything comes easy to you it's probably because someone else paid the price before you. It's not merely acknowledging your mistakes. It is being open to learn from your experiences as well. It breaks down walls that separate people because of title, position, or status. It encourages you to treat others as peers and not pawns in a story meant to make you successful.

SERIOUSLY?

I can answer this question with two words: Yes and No.

First the *Yes*.

You can take a vacation from leading others but there is no holiday when it comes to leading yourself.

Self-leadership is required at home, at school, at work, on a cruise ship, and on a sabbatical. This is serious business. That's why I've written this book. We're running out of leaders who take the idea and practice of leading yourself first seriously.

Does leadership start with you? Yes...seriously.

Now the *No*.

There's a difference between taking this process seriously and taking yourself seriously. Leading yourself first is a serious process. You'll be a much better leader if you do this. But taking yourself too seriously in the midst of the process is not my recommendation.

Look, you're going to mess up. You're not going to reach all your goals and some days won't go as planned. Even with the best of intentions, you'll find a way to make a mistake - especially if you're trying to improve and grow.

Learning to lead yourself first is no laughing matter. Learning to laugh at yourself is a characteristic of the best leaders.

If you learn to laugh at yourself, you will never cease to be entertained.

Og Mandino, one of the most prolific authors of the 20th Century, offers his own version of this powerful principle:

> "Laugh at yourself and at life. Not in the spirit of derision or whining self-pity, but as a remedy, a miracle drug, that will ease your pain, cure your depression, and help you to put in perspective that seemingly terrible defeat and worry with laughter at your predicaments, thus freeing your mind to think clearly toward the solution that is certain to come. Never take yourself too seriously."

You may not feel like your life is a laughing matter. That's okay. It may take some time for you to learn to laugh at yourself. Don't laugh at yourself during those times you feel good, learn to feel good because you laugh at yourself. Your example will inspire others to put aside their serious demeanor and laugh at themselves. The Rhodium Rule applies here as well.

I can think of no better way to end this book then to encourage you to laugh more, especially at your own shortcomings and idiosyncrasies. By all means, do the work necessary to grow and improve. Don't give in to the fatal flaws that trip up so many leaders. But find the joy in the process.

When you laugh at yourself, those whom you lead will laugh with you, near you, and perhaps, even at you (but that's okay).

People don't like to follow leaders who are overly obsessed with the importance of their own life story.

So lighten up. If you can't laugh at yourself, life's gonna seem a whole lot harder and a whole lot longer than you'd like.

And remember, just like everything else in this book...it starts with you.

ACKNOWLEDGEMENTS

It's hard to lead yourself, by yourself. It's also hard to write a book by yourself. Most everything I know I learned from someone else. I am a fortunate man to work with a lot of people who are smarter than me at my University.

Heartfelt thanks to all of the students who allow me the privilege of living my leadership out in front of them everyday. I am grateful for the input of my coworkers: Kenton Lee, Karen Pearson, Carey Cook, and Gene Schandorff, who always let me show them my next big project and pretend to act like they're proud of me.

I am indebted to the editing superpowers of Kathy Burns. She helped me put all of my words in the right place and pointed out better ones when necessary.

In the end, no one is truly an author until someone takes the time to read the words that are written. Thank you for letting me speak into your life through these pages. It means more than you know.

ABOUT THE AUTHOR

Tim Milburn currently serves as the Director of Campus Life at Northwest Nazarene University, located just outside of Boise, Idaho. He is the founder of Lifelong Leaders – an organization that inspires people to take responsibility, develop relationships, and achieve results.

Having worked with students for more than 25 years, Tim continually writes, speaks, and creates resources to empower student leaders and equip those involved in the work of student leadership development.

When he's not developing lifelong leaders, Tim dabbles in graphic design, is a regular at Starbucks, and loves to tell a good story.

To continue the conversation...

 On the web: **timmilburn.com**

 On email: **timothymilburn@gmail.com**

 On twitter: **@timage**

 On facebook: **facebook.com/timage**

Made in the USA
Lexington, KY
20 May 2015